SALMON

*I would like to thank my wife and son Elizabeth and Alasdair for their support and forbearance,
Des Thompson for his encouragement throughout and finally my father for making it all possible.*

First published in Great Britain in 2000 by
Colin Baxter Photography Ltd
Grantown-on-Spey
Moray PH26 3NA
Scotland

WorldLife Library Series

A CIP Catalogue record for this book is available from the British Library.

ISBN 1-84107-040-8

Photographs © 2000:

Front cover © Jeff Foott (BBC Natural History Unit)
Back cover © Laurie Campbell
Page 1 © Michael Quinton (Minden Pictures)
Page 3 © Paul Nicklen (Ursus Photography)
Page 4 © Jeff Foott (Auscape)
Page 6 © Harry M Walker
Page 8 © Sue Scott
Page 11 © Kennan Ward
Page 12 © Tom Walker (Planet Earth Pictures)
Page 15 © Michael Quinton (Minden Pictures)
Page 16 © Renée Kitt DeMartin
Page 19 © D. Parer & E. Parer-Cook (Auscape)
Page 20 © Renée Kitt DeMartin
Page 23 © Ken Sawada
Page 25 © Sue Scott
Page 26 © Paul Nicklen (Ursus Photography)
Page 29 © Bryan and Cherry Alexander
Page 30 © Jeff Foott (Auscape)
Page 33 © Hiromi Naito (Ursus Photography)

Page 34 © Jeff Foott (Bruce Coleman)
Page 36 © Art Wolfe
Page 37 © Jeff Foott (Bruce Coleman)
Page 38 © T Kitchin & V Hurst (NHPA)
Page 40 © Deni Brown (Oxford Scientific Films)
Page 43 © Ken Sawada
Page 44 © Kevin Schafer (NHPA)
Page 47 © Bryan & Cherry Alexander
Page 48 © Tom Walker (Planet Earth Pictures)
Page 51 © Kevin Schafer (NHPA)
Page 52 © Glyn Satterley
Page 55 © Laurie Campbell
Page 57 © Harry M Walker
Page 58 © John Shaw (Bruce Coleman)
Page 61 © Daniel J Cox (Oxford Scientific Films)
Page 62 © Laurie Campbell
Page 63 © Michael Roggo (Still Pictures)
Page 64 © David E Myers (Tony Stone Images)
Page 67 © Jeff Foott (Bruce Coleman)

Printed in China

SALMON

John M Baxter

Colin Baxter Photography, Grantown-on-Spey, Scotland

Contents

Introduction

Remarkable, awe-inspiring, mysterious: salmon are all of these and much more. In the North Atlantic the Atlantic salmon is supreme, with populations returning to rivers in many countries bordering the North Atlantic from Canada, Russia and Iceland in the north, to Scandinavia and the U.K., and as far south as Spain and Portugal. In the North Pacific there are six species of Pacific salmon that have various ranges from Japan and California in the south, to Arctic Russia and Alaska in the north.

Among the native peoples of many countries where salmon occur there are associated traditions, many of which stretch back into the mists of time. Without the salmon, the native peoples of the Pacific coastal regions could not have survived. They believed that only if the salmon were treated with respect would they continue to return. Thus rituals such as the 'First Salmon Ceremony' developed to pay tribute, and offer thanks to the salmon for returning yet again and ensuring the survival of the people.

On many parts of the coast of North America, people still practice the First Salmon Ceremony. Elsewhere, however, the ever-increasing pressures from the commercial exploitation of this valuable natural resource are demanding more and more of the sockeye and its cousins, which continue to return to their natal rivers year after year to spawn in their millions.

Similarly, the Atlantic salmon, often referred to as the 'King of Fish', is held in the highest esteem as both a valuable natural resource and a source of inspiration. Henry Williamson captured the essence of its life history in his saga *Salar the Salmon*. It has also been the subject of poetry and fiction, such as John Buchan's *John McNab*, and it is the substance of many apocryphal tales.

This book is a celebration of the salmon's majesty and their tragedy, and in some small way a tribute.

The classic image of a salmon in its relentless quest to reach the spawning grounds.

Salmon of the World

Salmon are members of one of the most primitive groups of bony fish. Modern-day salmon fall into two genera; *Salmo* – which includes the Atlantic salmon (*Salmo salar*), the brown trout, (*Salmo trutta*) and the rainbow trout (*Salmo gairdneri*) and *Oncorhynchus* – which includes the six species of Pacific salmon (chum salmon, *O. keta*; pink salmon, *O. gorbuscha*; sockeye salmon, *O. nerka*; chinook salmon, *O. tshawytscha*; coho salmon, *O. kisutch* and masu salmon, *O. masou*).

Pacific salmon and Atlantic salmon are sufficiently similar, both in appearance and ecological characteristics, that in the past there has been considerable debate as to whether they all belonged to a single genus or not. Although the distinguishing features that separate *Salmo* and *Oncorhynchus* are no longer in question they are undoubtedly closely related and their evolutionary sequence is well understood.

All seven species of salmon are to various degrees anadromous; that is, they undergo a migration from their natal freshwater river or lake out to sea, only to return to their freshwater origins to breed, and often to die. Within this basic life history, however, there are subtle variations in the timing of key events and habitat requirements of the different species.

It is generally assumed that the evolutionary ancestors of modern-day salmon were freshwater fish. The basic salmoniform fish is of great antiquity – at least 180 million years old. The Atlantic salmon is the most primitive and the various Pacific salmon have evolved, relatively rapidly, over the last six hundred thousand to one million years (during the Pleistocene epoch) from an ancestral Atlantic salmon stock. Towards the end of the Pliocene, around two million years ago, the Pacific and Atlantic Oceans were connected across what is the present Arctic region. This connection is borne out by the presence of many animal species in both the Pacific and Atlantic Oceans, but not so for *Oncorhynchus* and *Salmo*. This connection was then lost and throughout the Pleistocene, despite fluctuating sea levels due to advancing and retreating ice ages, it was never re-established.

Journey's end. An Atlantic salmon at the headwaters of the River Avon, Scotland.

As with all evolutionary history we can only speculate on what actually occurred but it would seem that the initial separation of the stocks of *Oncorhynchus* from the ancestral *Salmo* took place not later than the early Pleistocene.

In and around the indented coastline of the Asiatic margins of the Pacific Ocean, large areas of enclosed brackish waters formed as a result of land and sea-level changes. In these isolated water masses, rapid evolution of species occurred and it is here, probably in what is now the Sea of Japan, that the evolution from a far-flung stock of *Salmo* into *Oncorhynchus* began. With the reconnection of the enclosed waters of the Sea of Japan to the rest of the Pacific Ocean, this new, distinct stock, whether or not as yet a fully-fledged genus, was able to extend its range. Throughout the Pleistocene there were repeated appearances and disappearances of land and ice barriers in the North Pacific. These barriers resulted in the creation of other isolated bodies of water that persisted for anything between 50,000 and 100,000 years. Within these waters *Oncorhynchus* underwent further divergences, creating the different species that we see today.

The evolutionary history of Pacific salmon can be traced based on ecological, physiological and biochemical characteristics. The masu salmon is the most primitive and closely related to the Atlantic salmon; it is largely confined to coastal waters around the Sea of Japan. It is believed that some male masu salmon that mature in fresh water survive after spawning. The other five species show varying degrees of divergence: the chinook and coho salmon have marked similarities and remain quite distinct from pink and chum salmon which are themselves closely related. Physiological and behavioral similarities between pink and chum salmon, suggest that the two species diverged relatively recently in the evolutionary timescale. The sockeye salmon is the most distinct species and occupies an intermediate evolutionary position between the chinook/coho pairing and the pink/chum pairing.

Chum salmon *Oncorhynchus keta*

The name 'keta' is derived from the language of the Nanai people who live in the Khabarovsk and Primore regions of Russia, and literally means 'fish'.

Iridescent scales on the flank of a chinook salmon.

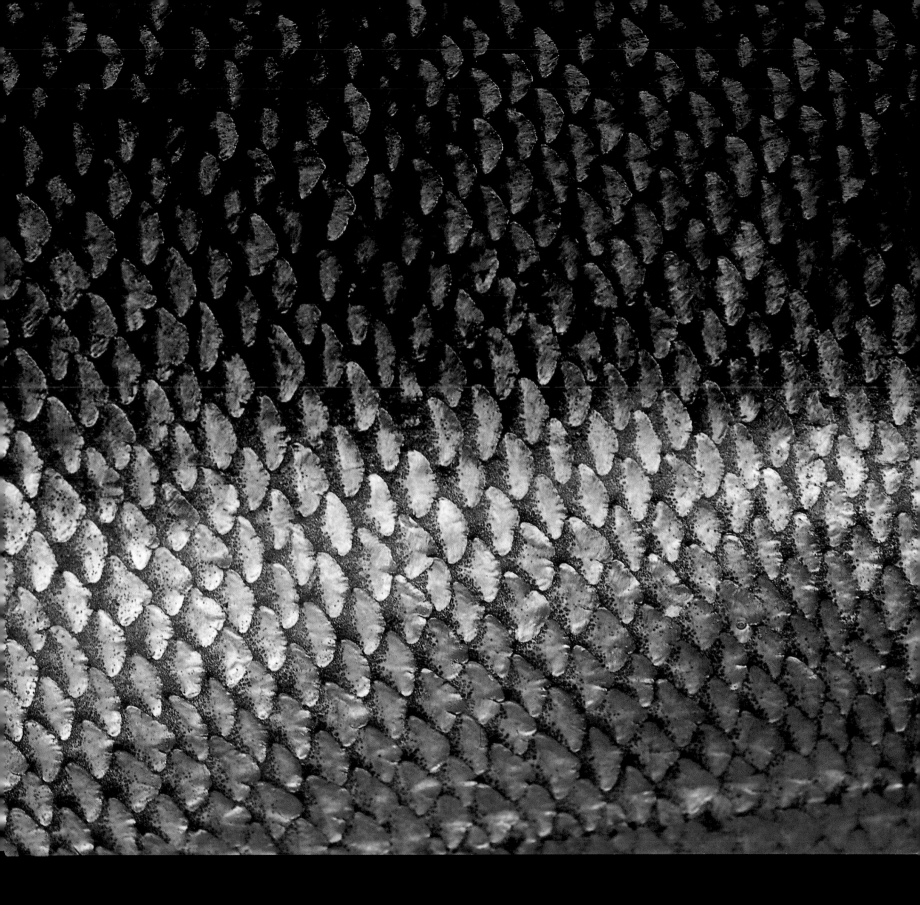

*Chum salmon in full spawning livery and displaying the large
canine-like teeth that earn them the vernacular name 'dog salmon'.*

The young fry have a green iridescence on their back with a series of slender, vertical bars (or parr marks) that extend only slightly below the lateral line. Adult fish can grow up to 43 in (109 cm) in length, and weigh as much as 44 lb (20 kg), although more typically they reach around 26–30 in (66–76 cm) and 9–13 lb (4–6 kg). They have a striking metallic-blue dorsal surface with occasional black speckling, the flanks are silver and all but the dorsal fin have distinctive dark tips. In fresh water maturing fish lose their metallic-blue sheen for a dullish green, and develop dark reddish streaks and pale blotches on their flanks, together with white tips to the pelvic and anal fins. Mature male fish develop large, canine-like teeth earning them the vernacular name 'dog salmon'. In Canada and the U.S.A. they are also known as the calico salmon, while in Russia and Japan there are many other regional names.

Chum salmon have the widest geographic distribution of all the Pacific salmon. They spawn in rivers stretching from north California through Oregon, Washington State, British Columbia and Alaska. In Arctic Alaska they are found in the Arctic Red and Peel Rivers, tributaries to the great Mackenzie River, and in the Slave and Hay Rivers that flow through the Great Slave Lake. On the Asian coast they occur as far south as Honshu through the Sea of Okhotsk, the Kamchatka Peninsula and Anadyr Bay to the Kolyma and Lena Rivers in Arctic Siberia. During their sea phase, chum salmon are distributed throughout the North Pacific above around 46°N and into the Bering Sea.

In years when there are large numbers of chum salmon the mean size of returning adults decreases, while the age of these mature fish increases. There is also marked competition between young chum and pink salmon: when young pink salmon are abundant, the survival rate of young chum salmon in coastal waters is lower; this pattern persists in the oceanic phase of their life. Conversely, during years when pink salmon numbers are lower, there are larger numbers of chum salmon.

Pink salmon *Oncorhynchus gorbuscha*
The fry of pink salmon are bluish-green along their back with silvery flanks and without any other markings. The adults are striking fish with an iridescent metallic-blue dorsal surface, silver sides and an opalescent white belly. The back, upper sides and caudal fin all bear

numerous large, black, almost oval spots. Mature males change in appearance, developing a very pronounced hump immediately behind the head and growing a distinct downward-pointing hook on the upper jaw. This change in shape has earned them the vernacular name of the humpback salmon. There is also a marked color change, with mature males developing red and yellow blotches on their sides and a general darkening on their back. The females undergo a similar change in coloration.

The pink salmon has a very large geographic spread; in British Columbia alone it is estimated that there are around 2200 separate spawning stocks. Pink salmon are found in the Sea of Japan from around the coast of Hokkaido, Japan, and the Tumen River, at the border between North Korea and Russia, extending northwards throughout the Sea of Okhotsk and Sakhalin Island, the Kamchatka Peninsula, the Bering Sea and the northern coast of Russia as far east as the Yana and Lena Rivers which flow into the Arctic Ocean. On the North American coast they extend from central California northwards around the coast, including the Aleutian Islands and reportedly as far east as the Mackenzie River in Arctic Canada, although recent surveys have not recorded any pink salmon from this system. The majority of the spawning stocks are confined to a band between 45°N and 65°N on both continents.

Pink salmon are the most numerous of the Pacific salmon species. In recent years the total annual commercial catch has been around 160 million fish, with west and east coast fisheries accounting for roughly 50 per cent each, the majority being caught by fisheries in the U.S.A. and Russia.

The pink salmon is the smallest of the Pacific salmon, typically reaching between 18 and 22 in (46 and 56 cm) in length and weighing between 3 and 5 lb (1.4 and 2.3 kg). A few pink salmon weighing up to 12 lb (5.4 kg) have been recorded but these are very much the exception. Pink salmon have a rigid two-year life-cycle and in many rivers and streams there is a two-year cycle of dominance, with either odd or even years consistently having much larger runs of fish.

The female pink salmon excavates the nest while the attendant male lies alongside.

Sockeye salmon *Oncorhynchus nerka*

Sockeye is a corruption of the name used by the native peoples of southern British Columbia – 'sukkai' – and its variants in the dialects of the Sooke, Snohomish, Comox, Saanich, Musqueam and Chilliwack. It is also known by other names in its range, including red salmon in Alaska, blueback salmon along the Columbia River, 'nerka' in Russia and 'benizake' or 'benimasu' in Japan. In addition to the vast numbers that migrate to sea each year there are also non-anadromous populations found in many lake systems. These are known as 'kokanee'.

Sockeye fry have an iridescent green, unmottled back with silver flanks and a white underside. A series of vertical dark parr marks run along each side extending only a short distance below the lateral line. The adult fish have a beautiful greenish-blue back with sparsely distributed fine black speckles. The flanks are brilliant silver. Maturing fish change color, in both sexes the head becomes olive green, the back and sides bright red, shading to darker red with green and yellow blotches more ventrally and white on the ventral surface. The male also changes shape, becoming laterally compressed and developing a pronounced fleshy hump in front of the dorsal fin.

The main sockeye spawning stocks have a relatively restricted range, due to their dependence on lakes for spawning and the initial growth of their young. On the North American coast they occur from around the Sacramento River in California to Kotzebue Sound. The main concentrations are found in the Bristol Bay watershed and the Fraser River drainage system of British Columbia, together with other systems such as the Skeena, Nass and Somass Rivers. On the Asian coast the main distribution is confined to around the Kamchatka Peninsula up as far north as the Anadyr River. Small numbers, however, are found as far north as Cape Chaplina and as far south as the north coast of Hokkaido and the Okhota and Kukhtoy Rivers, on the north-west coast of the Sea of Okhotsk in Russia.

In recent years catches of sockeye salmon have been in excess of 60 million fish, the majority being caught by Alaskan and British Columbian fisheries. Sockeye salmon flesh is darker red than other species, making it particularly appealing to the canning industry. Sockeye

A mature male sockeye salmon at the spawning grounds.

salmon vary in size depending on their river of origin. Fish from the Columbia River average only 3½ lb (1.6 kg), whereas those from the Fraser River average 6 lb (2.7 kg) and the largest are found in the Chignick River on the Alaska Peninsula, averaging 7 lb (3.2 kg).

Chinook salmon *Oncorhynchus tshawytscha*

The chinook salmon is also known as the spring salmon, king salmon or tyee (the Chinook word for 'large'); returning fish typically weigh up to 44 lb (20 kg). Fish of 99 lb (45 kg) are not uncommon and even larger fish are occasionally caught, such as a 126 lb (57 kg) fish measuring 53 in (135 cm) in length recorded in Petersburg, Alaska. There is an unofficial record of a fish weighing over 134 lb (61 kg).

Chinook fry have large, vertical, dark marks that extend well below the lateral line; the adipose fin (the small fleshy fin between the dorsal fin and the tail) is unpigmented except for a striking dark tip. Markings are, however, variable. Adult fish are greenish-blue on their dorsal surface mottled with large, irregular black spots that extend to the dorsal and caudal fins. In fresh water the maturing fish take on a dull dark greenish-bronze color. Uniquely, the adult chinook salmon has variable flesh color, from white through shades of pink to red, the color associated with all other salmon.

The chinook salmon is the least numerous of the five species of Pacific salmon that occur along the North American coast. Numbers have been declining steadily over many years, resulting in very low numbers in the mid 1980s, and although locally in some places stocks are gradually increasing, in many river systems spawning populations are still under serious threat.

There are around 1500 spawning populations of chinook salmon, the majority along the North American coast extending from the San Joaquim/Sacramento River system in California throughout the Aleutians and as far north as the Yukon River in Alaska. There are some, as yet unconfirmed, reports of chinook salmon in the Fraser and Coppermine Rivers in the Canadian Arctic. On the Asian coast spawning stocks are found from northern Hokkaido, all around the coast of the Sea of Okhotsk and the Bering Sea as far north as the Anadyr River.

Most of the spawning populations are small and potentially vulnerable to over-exploitation, and only a few, such as those in western Kamchatka, remain unexploited. Many

*An increasingly rare sight. The numbers of chinook salmon continue
to decline on most rivers and on many urgent action is needed to reverse this trend.*

spawning populations are estimated at less than 1000 spawners, but a few, particularly those at the extremes of the range, are much larger. On the Yukon and Nushagak Rivers, runs of between 400,000 and 600,000 regularly occur. The chinook salmon is the ultimate prize fish for anglers due to its large size. Approximately one million are caught each year in sports fisheries.

Coho salmon *Oncorhynchus kisutch*

The coho fry is a dull-gold color with around 11 narrow dark-brown parr marks on either side that extend equally above and below the lateral line. The fins are orange and the anal fin has a white leading edge with a parallel dark stripe. As the fry change into smolts (the stage at which salmon migrate from fresh water to the sea, somewhere between one and three years of age) they become more silvery, the fins change to a pale yellow and the dorsal surface takes on a greenish-blue tinge. Adult sea-going fish have a striking dark metallic-blue dorsal surface with irregular black spots, silvery flanks and ventral surface. As the fish mature on their return to fresh water, they undergo a dramatic transformation, with males changing to bright red, with a contrasting bright-green head and back, and a dark belly. The females take on a similar pattern but are much less strongly colored. In males the upper jaw forms an elongated hooked snout that may grow so large as to prevent the mouth from closing.

Adult fish average between 6 lb and 12 lb (2.7–5.4 kg), reaching around 22–26 inches (56–66 cm) in length; fish over 20 lb (9 kg) are rare and the heaviest ever recorded was a 31 lb (14 kg) fish caught off Victoria, British Columbia, in 1947.

Coho salmon return to many rivers and streams on the west coast of North America, from the San Lorenzo River north to Kotzebue Sound and Point Hope in Alaska. Their main centre of abundance is between Oregon and south-east Alaska. They are found scattered throughout the Aleutian Islands but have only a patchy distribution along the Asian coast where they are found in the Anadyr River, the southern regions of Kamchatka, the Sea of Okhotsk, Sakhalin, northern Hokkaido and Peter the Great Bay in Korea.

Throughout its range numbers are declining and some small spawning stocks are under

The perpetuation of the stock depends on these coho salmon successfully spawning.

threat of extinction. Coho salmon are a favorite of anglers, who account for a significant proportion of the total annual catch, which in recent years has been less than 20,000 tonnes.

Masu salmon *Oncorhynchus masou*

Masu salmon fry are a pale golden color, with a darker back mottled with bold black dots, and a series of vertical parr marks equidistant above and below the lateral line, which has a reddish tinge. The dorsal, pelvic and anal fins are tipped with white. The adult masu salmon have a steely black back, grading through silver flanks to a white belly. As mature masu return and enter their natal rivers their appearance changes; body color darkens and they develop a pattern of orange-red and olive markings. The upper and lower jaws of the male fish become hooked.

Masu are restricted to the Asian coast of the North Pacific. They are found from the south-eastern tip of Korea and Honshu up through Hokkaido, from Sakhalen to the Amur River in Russia and around the coast of western Kamchatka. The status of stocks throughout its range is not well documented. It is, however, a valuable fish although it accounts for only about 2.5 per cent (4000 tonnes) of the total catch of salmon by the Japanese fisheries. Adult fish average around 5½ lb (2.5 kg) in weight when they return to their natal rivers to spawn.

Atlantic salmon *Salmo salar*

The Atlantic salmon gained its name *Salmo*, which means 'the leaper', from the Romans, who encountered it in many of the rivers of northern Europe as they marched northwards almost 2000 years ago. The Atlantic salmon is known as the 'King of Fish' and has long been the prized quarry of both commercial netsmen and anglers.

Atlantic salmon parr have a silvery body with a row of parr marks like grayish-blue thumbprints along the body, straddling the lateral line, with a red spot between each. The back may also be dotted with brown or black spots, and the leading edge of the pectoral and pelvic fins is white.

When adult fish return from the sea they have dazzling silver sides and a silvery-white belly, and their back may be olive-green to dark blue. The greatest prize for any angler is to

Salmon are a prized catch for anglers around the world, regardless of whether
they are the mighty chinook, spring-run Atlantic salmon or this small stream-type masu salmon.

catch a salmon soon after it has entered the river, and it can receive no higher accolade than to be revered as 'a bar of silver'. As they mature in the river prior to spawning, the silver fades and they take on a bronze-pink color. Cock fish may darken further with time to a mottled pattern of brown, red and purple, often with red spots – an appearance that leads to the most colored fish often being referred to as 'tartan fish'. The lower jaw of the cock fish also develops a pronounced hook or 'kype' and the whole skull elongates. As females mature they too lose the silver color, taking on a dull purplish sheen with red spots.

Unlike Pacific salmon, some Atlantic salmon survive after spawning, reverting to a silvery appearance, but are rather thin and flaccid. These fish are known as kelts and some manage to return to the sea where they regain their condition, before migrating again to spawn.

Atlantic salmon average between 23½ in and 29½ in (60 and 75 cm) in length and weigh 6–10 lb (2.7–4.5 kg). Salmon that have spent only one winter at sea before returning to spawn are known as grilse and may weigh as little as 2 lb (0.9 kg). Some fish may weigh up to 48½ lb (22 kg), but these are increasingly rare (fish in excess of 22 lb (10 kg) are considered large). The record for a rod-caught salmon in Scotland is 64 lb (29 kg). The world record is held by a 79 lb (36 kg) fish caught in Norway in 1925.

Atlantic salmon occur on the east coast of North America as far south as the coast of Massachusetts but only in very low numbers. They occur along the entire coast of Newfoundland, extending north through Labrador. The Kapisigdlit River is the only river in Greenland that has a salmon spawning population. Iceland and the Faroe Islands support numerous spawning populations. Atlantic salmon occur as far south as the coast of Portugal and Spain and extend northwards including the Baltic Sea coast and the U.K., reaching their north-eastern limit in the Pechora River in Russia which empties into the Barents Sea.

Catch figures have shown a steady decline over the last 25 years, although in recent years this has been due in part to a reduction in fishing effort. In 1998, the reported total global catch of Atlantic salmon was 2401 tonnes.

Atlantic salmon stocks are showing serious signs of decline with fewer and fewer returning to spawn each year. In some places they are already locally extinct.

Salmon Life-Cycles

Young salmon leave their natal freshwater rivers and lakes, to go to sea to feed and grow, having spent anything from only a few weeks to several years as fry or parr (juvenile fish). Some years later and after traveling thousands of miles, they return to their home rivers as adults to reproduce, and in many cases to die. Atlantic and Pacific salmon share a common, basic life history although each species has evolved particular variations. A binomial convention has been adopted to indicate the age of salmon and the division of their life between their juvenile, freshwater phase and their oceanic phase. The pink salmon has a very strict two-year life-cycle, described by the binomial system as 0.1 (i.e., it migrates to sea within months of hatching and then spends one winter at sea before returning to its natal river the following summer to spawn). Other species have much more variable life histories; the sockeye may vary from 1.2 (i.e. it remains in fresh water for one winter and then migrates to sea, where it spends a further two winters before returning to spawn) to 2.3. During their upstream migration salmon do not feed, and they rely on body reserves built up while at sea.

Chum Salmon

There are two major groups of chum salmon, distinguished by the timing of their homeward freshwater migrations. Summer-run chum migrate into fresh water during July and August, autumn-run chum from late August through to October. In Asia summer-run chum salmon are native to Kamchatka, the Okhotsk coast, the Amur River and the east coast of Sakhalin, while autumn-run chum are native to Japan, the west coast of Sakhalin, the Kuril Islands and the Amur River. The Amur River is the only major river with both summer and autumn runs.

In North America there are also distinct summer and autumn runs although the pattern of distribution is less precise; in general, fish returning to more southern rivers tend to arrive later. In many rivers in Alaska, such as the Kobuk and Noatak, there is a single run in July and August. The Yukon River receives a very early run in May and June and then an autumn run

Such shoals of mature sockeye were once commonplace – now they cannot be taken for granted.

in September through to November. In British Columbia the runs on the Fraser, Chilliwack and Harrison Rivers occur between November and January.

Once chum salmon arrive in the estuary or at the mouth of their natal river after spending one to five winters at sea they mill around awaiting their cue to ascend. Increased water flow is the main stimulant for beginning this last part of their return journey. On arrival in the spawning streams after traveling hundreds of miles upstream, the female selects a nest area in relatively shallow water, about 12 in deep (30 cm), immediately above a turbulent, streamy area or where there is upwelling with a suitable gravelly river bed. She excavates a nest by violently flexing her body; during which time the male courts her. After creating a hollow between 8 and 16 in deep (20 and 41 cm), the female is ready to lay her eggs and the male lines up beside her so that they are immediately fertilized. The female begins to bury the fertilized eggs almost at once. Each female will excavate up to four or five nests, each one upstream from the last, and lay an average total of 2000–4000 eggs. She then guards the redd (nest site) from other females who might still be looking for a suitable place to spawn, until she dies some ten days later. Male salmon may fertilize the eggs of a number of females, until they too succumb and die on the redds.

The eggs hatch after around four months, and these tiny fish are dependent on their yolk sac for nutrition and are known as alevins. They remain in the gravel for about a month until they emerge as fry and immediately migrate towards the sea. The juvenile chum may spend a few weeks in the estuary feeding and growing, before venturing further into the near-shore marine environment. North American juvenile chum salmon are found along with juvenile sockeye and pink salmon, in a narrow coastal strip up to 22 miles (35 km) offshore, moving steadily westwards. Chum salmon are distributed over an extensive area of the North Pacific and Bering Sea. Asian chum salmon have been found as far east as 140° W, while North American chum do not tend to migrate so far and are not found west of 175°E. During the autumn and early winter there is a southerly migration that is reversed the following spring for those fish not destined to return to their natal rivers later that year.

The competition for suitable nest sites can be intense.

Pink salmon in the shallow margins of streams present an easy target for predators such as bears. As they mature, the males develop a pronounced hump on their back.

Pink salmon

Pink salmon congregate in bays and estuaries between June and August, having spent their last 15–18 months at sea. During daylight hours they travel up river to their spawning streams. On the Amur River in Russia, they travel anything from 124 to 435 miles (200–700 km) upstream. On the Fraser River they travel around 155 miles (250 km) and on the Nushagak River system in Alaska most travel around 124 miles (200 km) upstream. In years when very large numbers of pink salmon return to spawn, some fish will travel further than normal in an attempt to find unoccupied redds in which to spawn.

As they mature the males develop a pronounced hump on their back, an enlarged head and a downward-pointing hook on their upper jaw. It is thought that the hump may restrict the pink salmon from spawning in the shallowest margins of rivers and streams, the areas that are the first to dry up during periods of low flow or that freeze in winter. The hump might also attract predators, reducing the chances of female pink salmon being taken and ensuring the maximum number of eggs are laid.

Pink salmon spawn during September and October in relatively shallow, quite fast-flowing water over clean gravel. The female digs a nest by turning on her side and flexing her body, so moving stream bed material away, to form a shallow nest between 23½ in and 59 in (60–150 cm) in width and 39–98 in (100–250 cm) in length. Usually, at around dusk the female sheds some of her eggs into the nest and these are immediately fertilized by the attendant male. The female then moves just upstream of the nest and begins to dig rapidly. The disturbed gravel is carried downstream and fills in the nest containing the recently fertilized eggs. She may repeat this process up to four times and on average will lay between 1200 and 1900 eggs. During the construction of the redd a 3–4½ lb (1.4–2 kg) pink salmon may move up to 220 lb (100 kg) of gravel. After completing the redd she continues to defend it against other females, still digging their nests, until she dies some ten to thirteen days later.

The fertilized eggs buried in the gravel develop and hatch into alevin measuring ⅘ in (20 mm) that then grow into fry measuring 1¼ in, (31.8 mm) by the time they are ready to emerge five to eight months later. Pink salmon fry emerge at night and migrate quickly downstream at the surface, often in large schools; on any particular river the majority of the fry migrate within a period of only ten to twenty days. Six ocean migration patterns have been recognized for pink salmon stocks depending on their region of origin; Puget Sound and British Columbia; south-east, central and south-west Alaska; Bristol Bay and western Alaska; eastern Kamchatka to the Anadyr Gulf; western Kamchatka and the Sea of Okhotsk; and the Sea of Japan. Each pattern is discrete but with some overlap between adjacent stocks; in each the salmon move in an anticlockwise circular pattern. Although they complete the circuit only once, they may travel in excess of 4350 miles (7000 km). Pink salmon start their final homeward migration in May to July, having grown to between 3¼ lb and 5 lb (1.7–2.3 kg) in weight.

The precise two-year life-cycle of pink salmon (0.1) has resulted in odd and even year brood lines. In some stocks one year can be dominant and the other weak, in other stocks each year is equally abundant. Across wide geographic ranges, odd or even year brood lines are genetically more similar than the odd and even year's lines within a single stream. This has prompted the suggestion that odd and even year pink salmon stocks evolved separately from two isolated populations many thousands of years ago.

Sockeye salmon

Sockeye salmon are divided into a large number of stocks. On a single river different stocks show remarkable consistency from one year to the next in the timing and chronology of their return migrations.

Sockeye salmon spawn in a wide variety of habitats although a particular stock is loyal to a specific spawning area, which may be the headwaters of a river, a tributary, a river between lakes or the shallow areas of lake margins. The sockeye is the only salmon to spawn extensively around lake shores. Wherever they spawn, however, it is typically adjacent to a lake, which is necessary for rearing the juvenile stages. There are exceptions to the dependence on lakes for fry rearing, such as on the Kamchatka River, where the juveniles overwinter in springs and in creeks that do not freeze over, and the Stikine River at the border between Alaska and British Columbia. Unusually, on the Harrison River in British

Only a small number of the millions of eggs laid hatch into alevins, and then survive to return as adults.

Columbia and the East Alsek River, Alaska, the newly emerged juveniles migrate to sea almost immediately. Despite the lack of lakes these rivers support large runs of sockeye salmon. The East Alsek has as many as 180,000 returning adult sockeye salmon per year.

Sockeye spawn between late summer and autumn, the precise timing depending on local factors, most especially water temperature. Spawning takes place earliest in the north where a longer incubation is required due to the lower winter temperatures. In some lakes such as Iliamna Lake, Alaska, sockeye salmon spawn into coarse granite sand in water depths of 98 ft (30 m), while others in the same lake spawn over large angular stones too large for the salmon to move by their normal digging. In most places gravel beds with upwelling water are the preferred spawning habitat. Where possible a female will generally dig four or five nests each around 7½ in (19 cm) deep. Once a nest is dug the female and male sockeye lie side by side, and simultaneously shed their eggs and sperm. The nest is immediately filled in and the female then rests for several hours before digging the next nest just upstream from the last. On average a female sockeye will produce between 2000 and 2400 eggs; the older, larger fish, however, will produce many more. In digging her nests the female may move as much as 440–660 lb (200–300 kg) of gravel. Once the redd is complete the female remains on guard until her death between one and two weeks later.

After hatching, the alevin remain deep within the gravel bed and only once they have absorbed all the yolk sac and turned into fry do they venture out, at first during the hours of darkness. The fry move quickly downstream and enter the nursery lakes. Those salmon that emerge in lake outlet streams make an initial downstream migration followed by an upstream movement into the lake. Most juvenile sockeye will spend one or more winters in the lake before migrating to sea.

Some sockeye salmon remain in fresh water their entire life, maturing and reproducing without ever venturing to sea, although the origin of this behavior is unclear. These are known as 'kokanee' and are found in many lakes, some with runs of anadromous populations as well, such as the Fraser River drainage system. In other lakes there are resident kokanee

Returning sockeye salmon stocks converge on their natal rivers and display remarkable synchrony.

populations but no anadromous runs, such as lakes Whatcom, Sammamish and Washington in Washington State, and others in the Yukon, Kamchatka and on Vancouver Island. The kokanee resemble their anadromous cousins except for their smaller size at maturity. Where both kokanee and anadromous populations occur together, spawning is often segregated in time and space, with the kokanee generally spawning earlier in the year.

Sockeye on the spawning redds.

The seaward migration starts in spring and is often associated with the break-up of the ice on the nursery lakes. Vast shoals of smolts migrate seawards and can be almost as impressive a spectacle as that of the returning adults. The number can be mind boggling: the seasonal migration from Lake Iliamna in south-western Alaska has been estimated at 270 million sockeye smolts, with the majority of those leaving the lake over a period of only a few days.

Sockeye salmon may spend one to four years at sea. Different populations frequent different but overlapping sea areas. During the winter fish from Asia are found in the western North Pacific Ocean, as far south as 40°N; they then move northwards in the spring to the cold, rich waters of the northern Pacific and Bering Sea. Those returning to spawn move west through the Sea of Okhotsk, while those remaining at sea another winter move southward again onto the winter feeding grounds. Alaskan and North American populations display a similar anticlockwise migration, moving south in the winter, although not so far south as their Asian counterparts, and northwards in the summer. Asian and North American stocks intermix in the central North Pacific Ocean.

In early summer the fish destined to return to spawn that year are still spread over a vast area of the North Pacific Ocean. Some face journeys of over 1250 miles (2000 km) to

The ultimate sacrifice. The nutrients released from these decaying dead adult salmon will ensure the continued productivity of the stream needed to feed the emerging fry next spring, and so the circle is closed.

Waterfalls are a natural barrier that salmon, such as these chinook, have to overcome before they reach their journey's end. It may take many energy-sapping attempts for an individual to clear such a waterfall.

their natal rivers and lakes, others much less, but despite these differences members of particular stocks contrive to all arrive within a very short period of time.

Chinook salmon

Chinook salmon are very widely distributed, with over 1000 spawning populations in North America but fewer along the Asian coast. Spawning can occur from just above the tidal limits, up to the headwaters, which in some rivers, such as the Yukon, involves a migration of over 2175 miles (3500 km).

Chinook salmon are divided into stream-type and ocean-type populations. In Asia and Alaska all the populations are stream-type but from the British Columbia border south, there is a mixture of types in most rivers, with ocean-type populations dominating. Stream-type populations spend one or more years in fresh water before migrating to sea (1.x or >1.x) and then return in spring or summer a few months before spawning. The ocean-type fish migrate during their first year of life (0.x), normally within three months of emerging from the gravel, and only return to fresh water a few days or weeks prior to spawning.

Chinook salmon may be found returning to their natal river throughout the year although there are peaks at different times on different rivers. Northern rivers such as the Kamchatka, Yukon and Skeena have a single peak of returning fish around June. Rivers further south on the North American coast, such as the Fraser River where both stream-type and ocean-type fish occur, have two runs, with peaks in June and in September or October and sometimes a third much smaller peak in August. In most rivers one run tends to dominate, as is the case for the August peak on the Columbia and Klamath Rivers. In some rivers where there are two or three peaks, such as the Sacramento River which has a winter run as well as two earlier runs, there may be chinook salmon spawning throughout the year.

Chinook spawn in any suitable tiny tributaries and streams or main river channels. As with all other salmon species the female salmon selects an area of gravel bottom in relatively shallow water with a reasonable current, and digs a depression about 11½ in (29 cm) deep, into which she deposits some of her eggs, which are instantly fertilized and then covered over as a result of digging another nest upstream. This is repeated until all her eggs are laid. The number of eggs

varies with the size of the female, ranging from fewer than 4000 to over 14,000.

When the fry emerge from the gravel they travel downstream. Ocean-type fry move steadily downstream to the estuary, while their stream-type cousins stop and take up residence in the river for months, or a year, or more. The juvenile fish begin their seaward migration in the spring, remaining in the estuary for a few weeks, before venturing out into the more sheltered coastal waters during the summer, and then follow a general northward migration. Chinook spread out over an extensive area including the Bering Sea and the North Pacific south to 45°N. Most ocean-type fish do not disperse more than 620 miles (1000 km) from their natal river. Stream-type fish, however, have a much wider distribution throughout the North Pacific Ocean with chinook from Western Alaska occurring throughout the Bering Sea, and at least as far south as 40°N and as far east as 160°W. Chinook from Central Alaska extend throughout the north-eastern North Pacific Ocean.

Coho salmon

Coho salmon begin to arrive in their natal rivers during late summer and autumn, having traveled hundreds or thousands of miles. Successive generations of a stock appear in the estuary at around the same time each year. The start of the river migration is stimulated by high flow rates and often linked to a high tide. If conditions are not right, large numbers of coho salmon may be seen milling around in sea pools at the mouths of rivers and streams. In Alaska and Kamchatka the coho runs are in July and August, while in British Columbia they are later, in September and October, and in California they may be delayed until November or December. Overall the spawning run on any one river lasts up to three months; the earlier fish tending to migrate further upriver.

Coho salmon migrate upstream during the day and are frequently seen leaping out of the water. They move quickly through any rapids or shallow riffles, resting in the deeper pools before moving further upstream. Coho salmon seldom migrate further than about 155 miles (250 km) upriver into small streams and tributaries. Notable exceptions, however,

Juvenile salmon, like these coho, congregate in shoals where there is safety in numbers.

include the Skeena and Fraser Rivers in British Columbia, the Kamchatka River where they travel over 340 miles (550 km), and the Yukon River where they migrate about 1250 miles (2000 km), upstream. Coho salmon typically spend one winter at sea, returning to spawn in their third year of life, although they exhibit a wide range of life histories from 0.1–0.3 to 2.0–2.3. Returning coho salmon weigh on average 6½–7¾ lb (3–3.5 kg) ranging from 2½–15 lb (1.1–6.8 kg). Some males mature very early at one or two years of age and may not even have entered the truly marine environment at all. These fish are known as 'jacks'.

Most coho salmon spawn between November and January. This late peak in spawning places the coho at an advantage over other species, such as the sockeye and chum. When the coho female digs her nest she may dig up other eggs, of other salmon, which are then destroyed or eaten; there is much less chance that her own eggs will suffer the same fate.

The female digs nests in the fine gravelly river bed over a period of a few days. At the moment she lays her eggs she arches her body downward. This is the cue for the dominant male to come alongside. They lie next to each other, mouths open, bodies quivering and the eggs and sperm are released simultaneously. In all an average female may lay up to 5000 eggs. After spawning the female continues to protect the redd for around two weeks until she dies.

The fry emerge in spring or early summer and congregate in schools, hiding during the day in shady backwaters. They gradually become more territorial, taking up station in the slack water behind logs or stones. As winter approaches those fry that have not migrated to sea move back into deeper slow-moving pools. Typically, juvenile coho spend one winter in the river but some may spend two, three or even four winters there before migrating seawards.

They remain in coastal waters for several months before moving in a general northerly direction as far as the Gulf of Alaska, returning southwards later in the year. Many coho salmon remain close to the shore for their entire marine life. Others move out into oceanic waters where both Asian and North American stocks intermingle.

Masu salmon

Masu salmon are restricted to the Sea of Japan and the Sea of Okhotsk. There are both anadromous (ocean-type) and non-anadromous (stream-type or Yamame) populations.

A returning mature female masu salmon may be attended by
a number of much smaller male Yamame each intent on fertilizing her eggs.

At sea young Atlantic salmon feed voraciously, doubling in weight each year.
Those that return to spawn after only one winter at sea are known as grilse.

Those fish that do venture to sea eventually return after one to three winters, arriving back in their natal rivers in the early spring. In Japan masu salmon are known as 'sakuramasu', meaning 'cherry trout' – due to the coincidence of the cherry blossom and the return of the adult fish. Having entered the rivers, they hide in the deep pools throughout the summer, waiting until spawning time approaches before migrating upstream to the spawning grounds in August and September. Masu salmon are relatively small fish. The smallest weigh only 1 lb (0.45 kg) and measure 13¾ in (35 cm) in length, although they can reach 11 lb (5 kg) and 27½ in (70 cm).

Their spawning grounds are the headwaters of large rivers or tributaries in shallow swiftly flowing waters. The female digs her nest in the riverbed and then lays her eggs which are immediately fertilized by an attendant male – either an ocean-type fish or a Yamame. Depending on her size the female may lay between 2000 and 4000 eggs, although female Yamame produce far fewer, averaging only 200–300 eggs. She will then protect the nest for a few days before dying. Some Yamame survive and spawn again the following year.

The eggs hatch in late November or December and the alevins spend the winter in the gravel before emerging the following spring. Newly emerged fry spend some time in dense shoals before dispersing and moving downstream. Most ocean-type fish spend a year in fresh water before migrating to the sea.

Shoals of smolts migrate to sea between April and June, or later in some of the more northern rivers. The young masu are confined largely to coastal waters and relatively little is known about their wider distribution. Immature masu do occur in the Sea of Okhotsk but whether they venture into the Pacific Ocean and the Bering Sea remains largely a mystery.

Atlantic salmon

The Atlantic salmon is found in rivers of most countries bordering the North Atlantic Ocean. Fish return from the sea, entering their natal rivers throughout the year, and are known as spring, summer or autumn fish. Many rivers receive more than one run of fish, although in most one or another predominates. In Scotland, the Rivers Dee, Tay, Spey and Helmsdale traditionally receive a large early spring run. The Tweed receives a large, late autumn/winter run. Atlantic salmon may spend anything from one to three or even four winters at sea where they feed voraciously, doubling their weight with each year at sea. Those fish returning after only one winter are known as grilse and average around 5½ lb (2.5 kg).

Atlantic salmon return throughout the year, yet spawning takes place from October through to January/February; some salmon may have spent months in the estuary or river before finally maturing. Spawning takes place in the headwaters, tributaries or small streams with suitable gravel beds. The female digs a number of nests in the redd where she deposits her eggs, which are immediately fertilized before being buried maybe as deep as 6–12 in (15–30 cm). A 9–12 lb (4–5.4 kg) fish lays about 7000 eggs. Fish that have spawned drop back into the deeper pools where some die and others begin a passive journey back to the sea. At this stage they are known as kelts. Those that survive this journey begin to feed again, recovering enough for a small population to return to spawn a second time one or two years later. A very few even make a third successful spawning migration.

The eggs take 70–160 days to hatch, depending on water temperature. Alevins remain in the gravel for up to four weeks until they emerge as fry and quickly disperse to feed and grow into parr. Most remain in the river for one or two winters, but in the most northern rivers of Norway and Russia, where they grow very slowly, they may be seven years old before they migrate to sea. This migration generally occurs during spring and early summer. Where Atlantic salmon smolts went after entering the sea remained a mystery for a long time; although migration routes followed by North American stocks are well understood, even now little is known of the precise movements for European and Scandinavian stocks. In summer, concentrations of Atlantic salmon are found in the cold waters of the North Atlantic. In winter they move south and many are found off the coast of Newfoundland.

An Atlantic salmon attempts to leap a waterfall on its homeward migration.

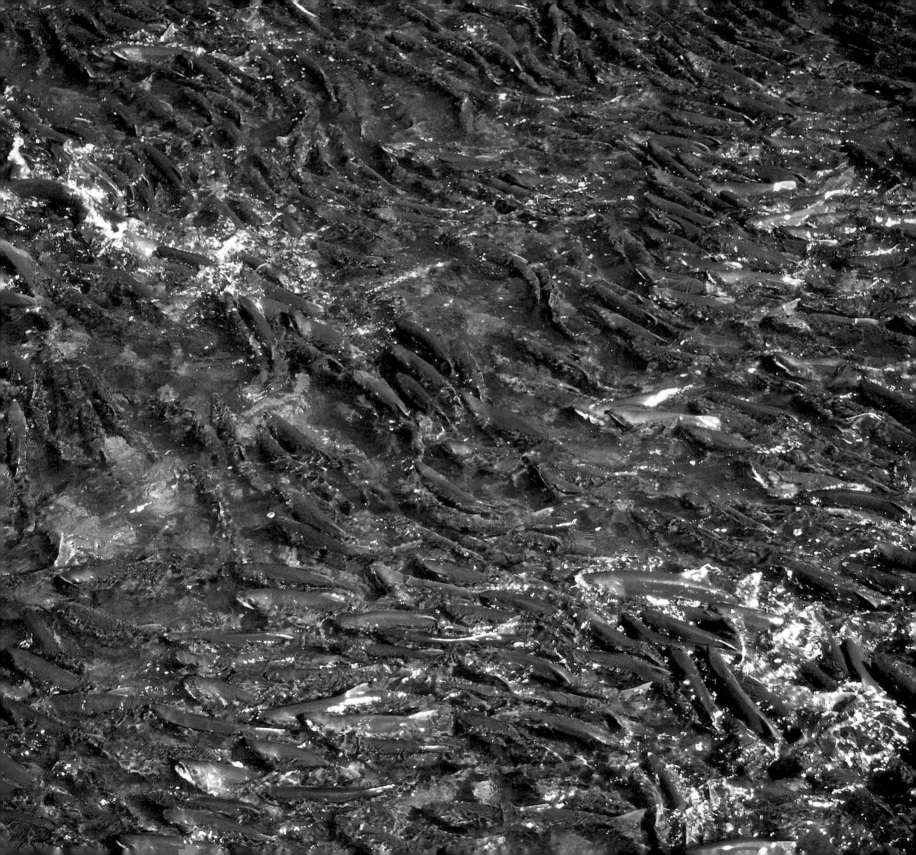

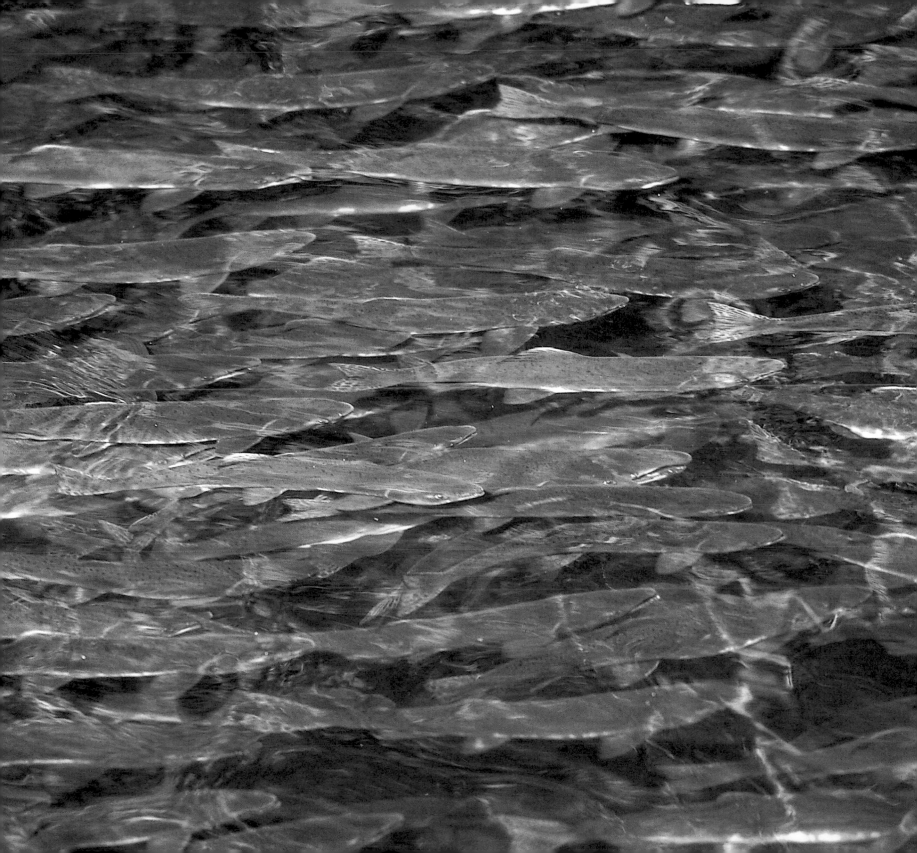

Fisheries

Both Atlantic and Pacific salmon have been a target of fishermen for centuries, for much of the time mainly confined to near-shore coastal and freshwater fisheries. Only in the last 70 years has there been any significant high-seas fishery that is controlled under international agreements. The present worldwide catch of salmon is around 1.5 million tonnes, with pink salmon accounting for 34 per cent, chum for 30 per cent and sockeye for 27 per cent. Many of these fish are the product of hatchery programs, and were released into coastal rivers and streams as fry; the native stocks long since proving incapable of supplying the demand for wild salmon. The total catch of Atlantic salmon in 1997 was estimated at 2400 tonnes, with Norway and Ireland accounting for 555 tonnes of this and the U.K. a further 500 tonnes, a tiny figure in comparison with the total production of Atlantic salmon by fish farmers.

On the west coast of America and Canada, salmon remain an integral part of the aboriginal culture. For the native people of the west coast, salmon were a staple source of protein. Estimates suggest that in the late 1700s, around 480 lb (220 kg) of fresh salmon were consumed per year per individual – a total annual consumption of about 195 million lb (88 million kg) in British Columbia alone. A complex culture of fisheries management developed to protect this natural resource, with individual villages being responsible for ensuring particular spawning streams were kept clear of blockages. On the Fraser River in the late 1700s between 50 and 100 million sockeye salmon alone, not to mention the pink, chum, coho and chinook, made the return journey each year. Between 2 and 2.5 million were caught. Coastal peoples used reef nets (basically a net strung between two stationary canoes) to intercept the salmon. Further up river, trawl or bag nets were used. In the Fraser Canyon, where the river passes through steep walls of rocks with many rapids, fishermen would stand on 'family' rocks and use a dip net to scoop fish out of the water. In the uppermost reaches and many of the tributary streams traps and weirs were constructed.

Salmon were respected and only as many as were needed were taken. The estimated

Stake nets intercept Atlantic salmon as they travel along the coast in search of their natal rivers.

catch (two to four per cent of the total run – prior to commercial fisheries) compares to a current take of nearer 80 per cent of a reduced stock, many of which are hatchery reared.

In Scotland, rights to salmon fishing, whether in the sea, estuary or river, originally belonged to the Crown. The earliest records of conveyance of rights date back to 1124, when King David I granted rights to fishing on the River Spey to the Priory of Urquhart. Since then such rights have mostly passed out of Crown control. Among a wide range of nets and traps, the two most popular were sweep nets and cruives. Cruives were weirs, built across a river, in which there were gaps into which a trap could be set. This form of fishing is now rare although sweep nets and cobles (short, flat-bottomed rowing boats) are still used on a few rivers.

Other traditional methods remain in use locally. The haaf-net fishery on the River Solway involves a net mounted on a wooden frame about 16 ft by 5 ft (5 m by 1.5 m) with a long handle that the fisherman holds over his shoulder, the net streaming behind. Typically, a number of fishermen stand side-by-side, chest-deep in the water, facing into the current. As the tide rises the outermost man moves to the shoreward end of the line. When a fish strikes the net the fisherman lifts the lower lip of the net to prevent the fish escaping. Traditional coastal fisheries occur in many other countries. In Norway stake nets, bag nets (or kilenots) and bend nets are used, in France most salmon are caught using seine and draft nets. Along the eastern seaboard of Canada a range of methods including trap nets, pound nets and weirs have been employed.

Catches of Pacific salmon increased dramatically with the advent of the canning industry in 1866 on the west coast of North America. At the same time recreational fisheries have also steadily increased and now account for a significant proportion of the total catch of some species, especially chinook and Atlantic salmon.

High-seas fisheries developed using a variety of techniques, principally long lines, trolls and gill nets, with catches either being landed directly ashore or on to attendant motherships where they were processed. These fisheries reached their peak in the early to mid 1930s when record catches were recorded for most species. At that time in excess of 50 million sockeye salmon were caught, together with over 80 million chum salmon.

The advent of a high-seas fishery for Atlantic salmon off the west coast of Greenland and around the Faroe Islands in the 1960s coincided with the discovery of these oceanic

The netting rights on many Atlantic salmon rivers have been purchased by conservation organizations in the face of dwindling catches both by the netting stations and anglers further upriver.

feeding grounds. Between the mid 1960s and the mid 1970s consistently high catches of around 10,000–12,000 tonnes were reported. Since 1980, however, there has been a steady decline due to a reduction in high-seas fisheries, and the introduction of quotas and the purchase of fishing licences by conservation organizations. Whereas most coastal fisheries targeted specific salmon stocks and therefore enabled an assessment of the overall exploitation of individual populations, the high-seas fisheries were non-selective and cropped randomly with no control, limit or knowledge of the level of exploitation of particular stocks.

High-seas salmon fishing in the Pacific Ocean, and also fishing for Atlantic salmon in international waters, has been prohibited by international convention. Such controls are essential if individual stocks of salmon are to be managed effectively. Conventions, however, are not foolproof and so long as some states are non-signatories they are free to exploit these stocks in international waters. These are often countries that do not even have a native stock of salmon returning to their rivers and they have little vested interest in the long-term sustainable management of the salmon, preferring the short-term rewards.

Atlantic salmon stocks have declined to alarmingly low levels. Grilse are only just within safe biological levels and the larger fish that spend two or more winters at sea, especially those originating in southern Europe, including the U.K., are already outside the safe biological limits for the populations to be able to sustain themselves with an adequate genetic diversity. Similarly, many Pacific salmon stocks are protected, or are being considered for protection under the Endangered Species Act, with many native stocks already extinct. Current record catch levels are only maintained as a result of hatchery releases.

There is an urgent need for a radical approach to commercial fisheries management. Wider co-ordinated measures are also urgently required, that take into account a wide range of factors to ensure that native stocks can recover and continue to flourish. The efforts of organizations such as NASCO (the North Atlantic Salmon Conservation Organization) and its counterpart for the Pacific Salmon, NPAFC (the North Pacific Anadromous Fish Commission) are pivotal in this work.

Gill net fisheries still account for large numbers of Pacific salmon.

Trials and Tribulations

Throughout their life salmon encounter so many trials and tribulations that the vast numbers of eggs spawned each autumn are massively depleted to the 'relatively few' mature adults that eventually return.

These losses start even before the eggs have hatched. In the crowded redds, eggs laid by early spawning fish are disturbed by other salmon excavating their nests. Although such losses are serious for the propagation of the genetic material of those individuals concerned, they are of little consequence to the overall productivity of the redd, which has only a finite carrying capacity. These disturbed eggs are not wasted, but are eaten by scavengers such as gulls, terns and mergansers, together with various fish including sculpins, trout and charr. Severe floods and droughts, or periods of exceptionally low temperatures causing streams or lake margins to freeze over, can also take a serious early toll.

From the moment the eggs hatch and the fry emerge from the gravel they have to run an endless gauntlet of predators. The clouds of emerging fry provide a wonderful food resource for the juveniles of other salmon species as well as trout, sculpins and charr and birds such as dippers and goosanders. The very high densities of fry that are present during a relatively short period as they are emerging result in great numbers being eaten; as many as 80 per cent of the emergent fry may be lost at this time. As the numbers of young salmon decline and they grow in size, fewer are taken, although herons, goosanders and mergansers, together with mink and otters, continue to deplete their numbers.

At sea a new range of predators awaits including the salmon shark, porbeagle shark, Greenland shark and common skate, together with other fish such as halibut, ling, cod and pollack. Despite their name salmon sharks do not feed exclusively on salmon, although salmon do represent a high proportion of their diet. They feed on all species of Pacific salmon but in western North Pacific waters they mainly take pink salmon, and in the central North Pacific and Bering Sea it is sockeye and chum salmon that make up the largest proportion of their diet.

The ultimate fisher – a brown bear catches a sockeye salmon at a waterfall in Alaska.

Salmon are also eaten by various cetaceans including killer whales, humpback whales and Pacific whitesided dolphins. In the coastal waters of the Moray Firth around the mouth of the River Spey on the east coast of Scotland, a resident population of bottlenose dolphins feed on the salmon returning to this famous river. Salmon of all species fall prey to a range of different pinnipeds, including fur seals, harbor (or common) seals, gray seals and sea lions. Increases in seal numbers in recent years have created tension between fishermen, fisheries managers and conservationists with respect to what, if anything, should be done to control seal predation of salmon. It is a dilemma with no simple answer. Seals are highly visible and voracious predators and as such an ideal scape-goat to take the blame for declining salmon stocks. While it is undoubtedly the case that seals eat salmon there is little evidence to suggest that even a drastic reduction in seal numbers alone, such as some advocate, would halt the decline in wild salmon stocks, especially of the Atlantic salmon, that has been observed in recent years.

Even as the adult fish begin the final journey up their natal river to the spawning grounds they still have further obstacles to overcome. Very few rivers have escaped the impact of some human activity or other causing either directly or indirectly problems for the salmon. Many rivers have been dammed or had weirs built across them and can have a devastating effect on salmon runs. The River Elwha in the northwest of Washington State used to have a spawning run of around 400,000 salmon including the mighty chinook with specimens of over 100 lb (45 kg) not uncommon. Now as a result of two dams on the river a mere 3000 salmon return to spawn in the lower few miles of the river. This story is sadly not unique but in this case at least there is a glimmer of hope with the US Congress and the President backing a proposal for the removal of the dams together with a programme of river restoration at an estimated cost of around $115 million. In many instances such obstacles have been at least partially overcome by building fish ladders or lifts to enable salmon to pass and gain access to the upstream spawning grounds. Chum salmon, however, do not like the turbulent waters of fish ladders and will not ascend them. In addition to restricting access to the upper reaches of rivers, dams can also result in major alterations to the water flow

Chum salmon on the McNeil River, Alaska, have a series of small falls to ascend.

regime of the river. A regime that changes from one of spate to one of low flow in only a few hours, sometimes on a daily basis, makes it very difficult and confusing for salmon trying to reach the spawning grounds.

Rock slides, for example the case on the Skeena River in 1951, can block the passage of returning salmon. Natural disasters have always occurred but the increasing pressure that native stocks are under makes it more difficult for them to survive as a result. In other cases they are the indirect result of human activities, such as at the Hells Gate in the Fraser River canyon which was blocked by a massive slide in 1911 caused by railway construction nearby. Few sockeye salmon could reach their spawning grounds for a number of years. The blockage was eventually removed but the runs of sockeye salmon were very badly depleted for decades afterwards.

One that didn't get away.

Good water quality is essential for the continuing success of salmon runs. Many rivers have been gradually polluted over decades with some reaching such a state that salmon ultimately fail to return to spawn and the population is lost for ever. It is not only the salmon that suffer but the entire web of life of the river. Without the salmon many predators and scavengers are deprived of important sources of food often at critical times of the year. Other delicately balanced interdependencies, such as that of the parasitic glochidial (larval) stage of the European freshwater pearl mussel, itself an endangered species, on young salmon and trout, for sustenance and dispersal, are destroyed, thus threatening the continued survival of the mussel populations.

Pollution can take many forms, such as heavy metals resulting from mining activities, and a variety of compounds including chlorinated hydrocarbons, organo-phosphates, herbicides,

The production of farmed Atlantic salmon is close to 500,000
tonnes per year, needed to meet the increasing consumer demand.

Some salmon trying to jump the Brooks Falls in Alaska
are snapped out of mid air by hungry bears. A large brown bear
may consume as much as 110 lb (50 kg) of salmon in a day.

fertilizers and farm waste. At certain concentrations these can be lethal and the effect on salmon, and other fish, is immediate and dramatic. There are other more insidious non-lethal effects such as that of copper, which prevents salmon adapting to the physiological demands of living in seawater. There are some notable success stories, however, such as the River Thames in England where the water quality has been improved to such a degree that salmon are again returning to spawn.

The impacts of acidification on Atlantic salmon stocks were first evident in some Norwegian rivers even at the end of the nineteenth century. Salmon are particularly sensitive to acid water and there is now evidence that the effect is widespread, with reports of declining or vanished populations on rivers in Norway, Sweden, Canada, the U.K. and the U.S.A. Low pH can delay or prevent eggs hatching, and those that do hatch show reduced growth rates and high mortality rates. The rivers in the south of Norway and Sweden are most at risk, with many rivers either having very reduced stocks or no stocks at all.

As the salmon battle their way upstream they still have some predators to avoid. Otters and mink take smaller fish, but on many of the great salmon rivers of the west coast of North America and the east coast of Russia, the salmon represent a vital, late influx of high-quality protein to large numbers of black, brown and grizzly bears. These bears are expert fishers and compete for the best fishing stances on the river. Grizzly bears tend to feed in groups while brown bears prefer to fish in isolation, although in some circumstances they too will fish in groups. At certain locations this has created a wildlife spectacle to rival any in the natural world. On the Naknek River in the heart of the Katmai National Park, on the Alaska Peninsula, brown bears congregate at the 6½ ft (2 m) high Brooks Falls. Thousands of sockeye salmon have to scale these falls to reach their spawning grounds in Brooks Lake. The bears gorge themselves on this bonanza, snorkeling in the salmon-packed pools beneath the falls, or plucking salmon from the water as they struggle over the lip at the top. A large brown bear may consume as much as 110 lb (50 kg) of salmon in a day. The bears not only feed on salmon as they struggle upstream to their spawning grounds, but also take advantage of the easy pickings provided by the carcasses of the thousands of dead and dying fish that are left after they are finished spawning. Other scavengers also feast on the corpses of the Pacific salmon, including the Steller's sea eagle. These majestic birds gather on the Kamchatka Peninsula in the winter where up to 60 per cent of the total world population can be found around Lake Kurilsky, attracted by the large numbers of returning sockeye salmon.

The other great predators on salmon are humans who continue to hunt them up until their final arrival at the spawning redds. Subsistence fisheries continue, accounting for thousands of fish; but recreational anglers catch an even higher number. In Scotland almost 50 per cent of the Atlantic salmon total catch falls to anglers, and although the number of fish caught by anglers has decreased, it has increased as a proportion of the catch.

As our understanding of the biology of the salmon increases, it is becoming apparent that there are other much greater factors at work. Despite the tangible and obvious impacts of coastal predators, such as seals and man, and other local impacts on individual river stocks, the overall survival of the salmon is dependent on greater global oceanic factors. The declines in stocks of both Pacific and Atlantic salmon, which have accelerated in recent years, are linked to ocean temperature patterns. The effect of global warming on the behavior of major climatic events such as the North Atlantic Oscillation, has resulted in a warming along the southern extent of the main oceanic nursery areas, with consequent impacts on Atlantic salmon production and survival. These are not simple problems to solve but at least reinforce the need; for in trying to protect and enhance the natural populations of the salmon, the widest possible view must be taken of the challenge that we are now facing.

It would take a brave person to predict what we might be saying about the salmon in 50 years' time. It is almost unbelievable that we may be talking of them in terms of an endangered species but there are too many early warning signs for us to ignore them. The salmon are intriguing, remarkable, enigmatic but most of all glorious. They provide so many wonderful spectacles, from the ribbons of vermilion that are the returning sockeye salmon to the flashes of silver that are Atlantic salmon – the leaper.

We all have a responsibility to ensure that what is so much a part of the wealth of our global natural heritage is protected and conserved. They are kindred spirits.

The life-cycle of the salmon is one of constant renewal.

Salmon Facts and Distribution Maps

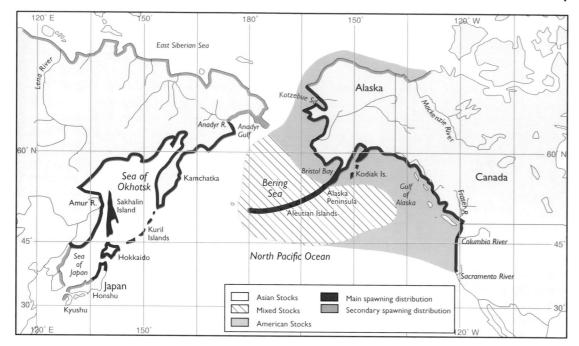

Chum Salmon

(calico or dog salmon)

Scientific name: *Oncorhynchus keta*

Adult weight: typically: 6 lb 8 oz–12 lb (3–5.4 kg)

Abundance: 2 (where 1 is highest)

Typical life history: 0.4 (maybe 0.2; 0.3; 0.5)

Breeding behavior: Anadromous

Distribution: *Asia*: Kyushu Island, Japan and Naktong River North Korea north to Anadyr River, Russia, but recorded as far west as the Lena River in the Laptev Sea.
North America: San Lorenzo River north to Kotzebue Sound, Alaska but as far east as the MacKenzie River, Canada.

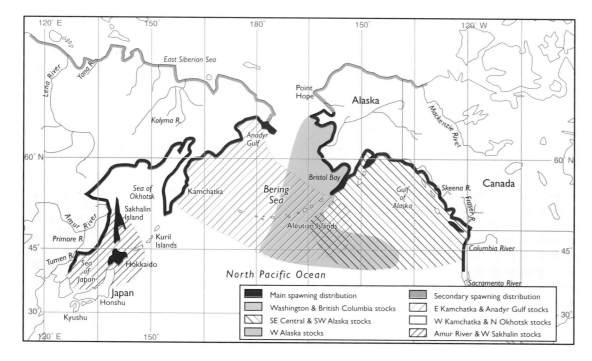

Pink Salmon

(humpback salmon)

Scientific name: *Oncorhynchus gorbuscha*

Adult weight: typically: 2 lb 3 oz–5 lb 8 oz (1–2.5 kg)

Abundance: 1

Typical life history: 0.1

Breeding behavior: Anadromous

Distribution:

Asia: North Korea and Hokkaido coast north to the Lena River, Russia.
North America: Sacramento River north to Point Barrow on Beaufort Sea coast although unconfirmed records extend this to the MacKenzie River, Canada.

Salmon Facts and Distribution Maps

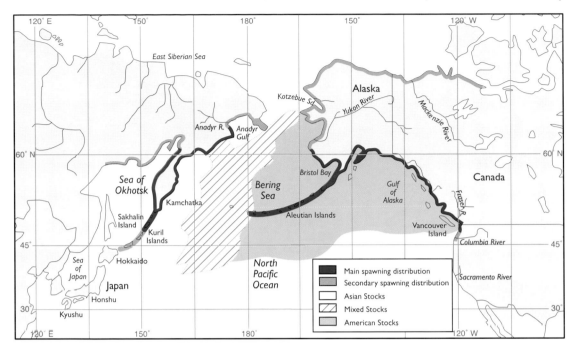

Sockeye Salmon

(blueback, red, nerka or benizake)

Scientific name: *Oncorhynchus nerka*

Adult weight: typically 6 lb 10 oz
(3 kg)

Abundance: 3

Typical life history: variable
(but most common are 1.2; 1.3; 2.2; 2.3)

Breeding behavior: Anadromous /
non-anadromous

Distribution:

Asia: From southern tip of the Kamchatka
Peninsula north to Anadyr River in Russia.

North America: Sacramento River north to
Kotzebue Sound in Bering Sea.

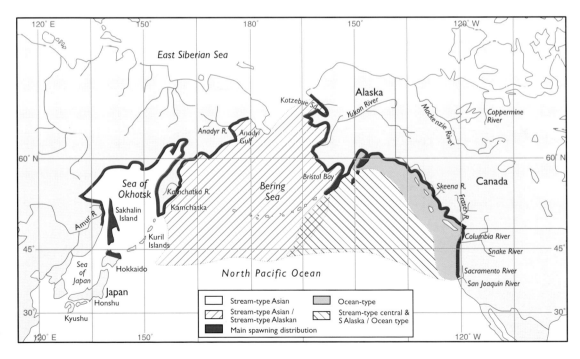

Chinook Salmon

(spring, king, Quinnat or tyee)

Scientific name: *Oncorhynchus tshawytscha*

Adult weight typically: 22–44 lb
(10–20 kg)

Abundance: 5

Typical life history: 0.1–0.5 Ocean type;
1.2–2.5 Stream type

Breeding behavior: Anadromous

Distribution:

Asia: Hokkaido north to Anadyr River,
Russia.

North America: San Joaquim/Sacramento
River north to Yukon River, Alaska.

Salmon Facts and Distribution Maps

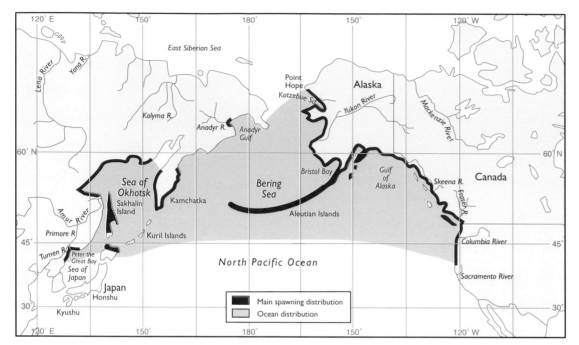

Coho Salmon

(silver salmon)

Scientific name: *Oncorhynchus kisutch*

Adult weight typically: 6 lb 10 oz–7 lb 11oz (3–3.5 kg)

Abundance: 4

Typical life history: 1.1 (varies inc. 1.0; 1.2; 2.0; 2.1)

Breeding behavior: Anadromous (some male fish 'jacks' may never enter the marine environment proper)

Distribution: *Asia:* Northern Hokkaido and North Korea and patchily north to Anadyr River, Russia.
North America: San Lorenzo River north to Point Hope, Alaska.

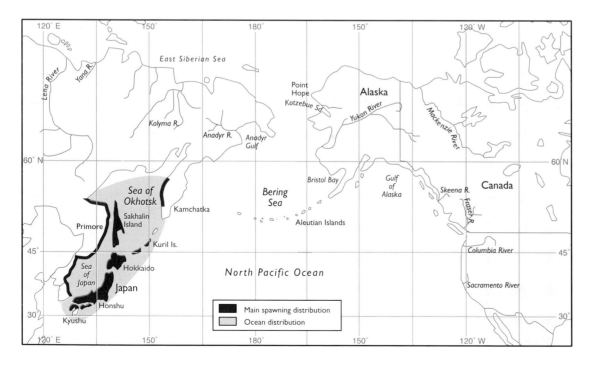

Masu Salmon

(Yamame, or sakuramasu)

Scientific name: *Oncorhynchus masou*

Adult weight: typically: 5 lb 8 oz (2.5 kg)

Abundance: 6

Typical life history: 1.1 (but varies from 1.2–3.3). Yamame 1.0 or 2.0

Breeding behavior: Anadromous / non-anadromous

Distribution:

Asia: Coastal areas of Sea of Japan and Sea of Okhotsk, south as far as west Honshu and south-east Korea, north to the Amur River and west Kamchatka.

Salmon Facts and Maps

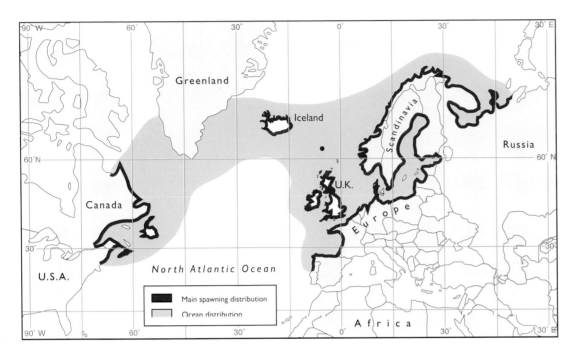

Common name: Atlantic salmon
Scientific name: *Salmo salar*
Adult weight typically: 6 lb–9 lb 14 oz (2.7–4.5 kg)
Typical life history: 1.1–2.3 (but exceptionally 6.1 or 6.2)
Breeding behavior: Anadromous
Distribution: *North America:* Massachusetts north to Labrador coastGreenland, Iceland and Faroes. *Europe:* Atlantic coast of Spain and Portugal in south to Pechora River in Russia, including the Baltic, U.K. and Scandinavia.

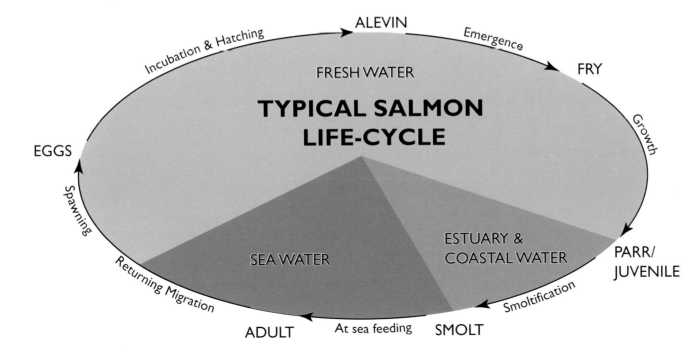

Index

*Entries in **bold** indicate pictures*

Recommended Reading

Ecology and Management of Atlantic Salmon, 1989, Derek Mills (Chapman and Hall).
The Atlantic Salmon, 1992, W.M. Shearer (Fishing News Books – Oxford).
Salmon – An Illustrated History, 1992, A. Barbour (Canongate, Edinburgh)
Pacific Salmon Life Histories, 1991, ed. C. Groot and L. Margolis (UBC Press, Vancouver)
Field Guide to the Pacific Salmon, 1992, R. Steelquist (Sasquatch Books, Seattle)
Salmon, Trout and Charr of the World – A Fisherman's Natural History, 1999, R. Watson (Swan Hill Press, Shrewsbury)

Biographical Note

John M Baxter is chief editor of the *International Journal of Aquatic Conservation* and has written widely on marine issues. He manages the Maritime Group in Scottish Natural Heritage and is series editor of the SNH *Living Landscape* series. Dr Baxter holds a Ph.D in zoology. He became involved in researching methods to monitor the impact of the North Sea Oil industry, before joining the Department of the Environment (N. Ireland). He returned to Scotland to take up his current post, as head of marine conservation in the government's nature conservation agency. He is a keen salmon angler.